Job Seeker's Ins.

Ignite Your LinkedIn Profile

A Job Seekers Guide to Get More
Leads, Referrals & Interviews and
Land a Great Job

Donald J Wittman

Contributing Author

Loretta A Stevens

ISBN:

978-1-7338059-1-9 (paperback)

978-1-7338059-2-6 (ebook)

DOWNLOAD THE AUDIOBOOK FREE!

Just To say Thanks for downloading my book, I would like to offer you the Audiobook version 100% FREE!

https://bit.ly/3mNijd6

I would like to dedicate this book to the following people:

My Parents

They have always wanted me to be successful with all the endeavors I have jumped into. My parents, growing up in the Great Depression, stressed the need to work hard. One of the big things that the Depression taught was that you need to keep friends and family close because they are all you have when things get bad. This passion for helping others came into focus when I consulted and learned how LinkedIn works. They understood that being out of a job was a challenging time and needed to help each other. My friends from the HERT and SERT Networking groups got me thinking about where I came from and that it was time to help others. It finally sank in, and I feel more in touch with people than I have ever been. So Mom and Dad, thank you for getting me to where I think I belong.

My Son, Stephen

Stephen has been a great help with this book. He helped me to focus on talking simpler and explaining more. It is difficult not to speak geek when talking about a subject like LinkedIn. I have spent most of my professional life getting straight to the point. I generally assumed that the people listening to me had enough background to get into the topic's meat. This is a massive mind-shift for me.

My Wife, Regina

Regina has been very tolerant and supportive of my going solo with my career change. We have had a great time traveling before this change. Her belief that things would get better has been a great lift for me when things look dim. I cannot thank her enough for her support.

Contents

Introduction

"Why isn't LinkedIn working for me?"

The simple answer is that very few people understand how LinkedIn works. Many of the free courses only address the initial setup of a LinkedIn profile. Even many of the paid courses out there don't do anything beyond the basics.

Many of the courses do not even tell you the basics. Some of the courses spend a lot of time on branding. Others work on making your profile look professional or teaching you how to use generic keywords. These steps are backward; these are the last things you should do, not the first things you should do.

The first thing you need to do is be visible to the recruiter; no one I have found is covering this. The second thing is to find current and specific keywords for the position you are looking for, not generic position keywords. Without these two, recruiters are not going to find you Via a LinkedIn search. After all, why are you on

LinkedIn if not to be found by a recruiter or potential client?

One of the best lines I have heard from LinkedIn professionals is that "we are just going to put your resume into your LinkedIn profile. Then, we will pretty it up a bit, and you will be good to go!" This line could not be further from the truth!

LinkedIn is a search engine. To make LinkedIn work, you have to feed it the information it wants to get the results you need. To use a good analogy, if you are going to cook a meal for your family, and you have all the ingredients but nothing to cook it with, you will have a problem with it coming out very well if at all edible, the same thing with LinkedIn. You can have the most beautifully written profile, but if you do not give LinkedIn the food it needs, the search for you will fail. Keywords are the food LinkedIn needs for the position you want, or you will not have the desired result. The result you want is to be found by recruiters. Most LinkedIn users find themselves in this problem.

When job seekers land their next job, the most common comment I have received is, "I will always be ready for my next position." The training and consulting I've done in the last seven years emphasize that "I will never, ever be unprepared for a potential jobless event again. My LinkedIn profile is always updated religiously."

I have had people prepare their LinkedIn profiles for the next potential position right after they have landed a job. This tells me how uncertain the job market is. With all the company buyouts and automation projects, the most stable companies are looking to size their staff efficiently. An extreme example is one of my clients in the medical device arena. He has looked for a new job every year for the last four years because of all the mergers and acquisitions in his industry. The other area is the outsourcing craze. Companies are saying, "If the business function is not critical to the success of the business, why are we managing it? Let's outsource it to allow the Company to focus on what is most important."

This is the introduction book to my Job Pull Strategy. This book will teach the value of building a searchable LinkedIn profile that ranks in search via both LinkedIn and Google. This book takes you through the basics of what you need to put in place to show up on the first page. It starts with the assumption that you have already set up a LinkedIn profile for yourself. We will begin by going over some LinkedIn background and statistics to understand better why we are doing this. We will then go through a LinkedIn profile checklist, which sets the stage to make everything work. We will then move into what affects LinkedIn visibility. We will cover how to find keywords for the position you want at a high level. Then, we will move on to identifying the high-value areas of a LinkedIn profile. Finally, we will do a profile search example to understand what we are doing.

I started out helping people with LinkedIn while I was searching for a new job myself. I ended up reverse-engineering how LinkedIn search worked. I tested my Keyword Strategy for many months. This Keyword Strategy allows me to put almost anyone in a job search on page 1 for the position they are seeking. I call this process my Job Pull Strategy System. Others may call it an Inbound Marketing Strategy or Pull Marketing Strategy.

My friends were my first guinea pigs as I developed this system. It was they who pushed me to build my webinar series and write this book. It is their positive results that gave me the confidence to put together my Company. My consulting business helps job seekers and small businesses move to the next level. I teach seminars for groups in New York City, Connecticut, and Massachusetts once a year.

One of these seminars had the potential to be canceled because of an impending snowstorm; several people emailed and asked whether we were having the seminar or not. They said that they would travel through the snowstorm rather than miss my seminar.

I am a recovering Chief Technology Officer who likes to help people positively. So digging into LinkedIn was a natural curiosity for me. Just like Google, LinkedIn is a search engine. The difference between LinkedIn and Google is that their search algorithms make different assumptions.

Most people who utilize the strategies outlined in this book have more "LinkedIn search appearances." Your "Who viewed your profile" appearances will also increase in your Linked-In Dashboard. These results are from my 30-minute follow-up calls after many of my webinars. Some professionals have very challenging positions that may need much more detailed help. They attend a more advanced seminar for

"More Powerful Search Ranking." Those who took this seminar had significant increases in their dashboard counts. These results are prevalent for those who apply my strategies. My seminars or books have no guessing; they lay it out for you in a simple-to-understand "how-to" method.

The strategy helps you walk through what recruiters are looking for when searching for a position they are trying to fill. Recruiters use a very straightforward technique.

Recruiters first search for:

- Job title

- Job attributes

- Keywords

- Company fit

The biggest thing that most people don't address is visibility. We go through what visibility is and how it affects your profile on LinkedIn later in the book. Without visibility on LinkedIn, it won't work no matter what you do to get traffic to your profile. So there are three things we're going to address in this book.

They are:

- Visibility

- Functional fit

- Company fit

You will see how these three things will dramatically change how your LinkedIn profile works. Then we will go over why you are not getting search appearances and see how the search appearances drive profile views. Current statistics tell us that it takes, on average, 1,000 general page views or 300 recruiter views to get a job offer. With this strategy, we will significantly enhance your ability to be found by a recruiter. In addition, it will help you understand what you have to do to make ongoing changes to adapt to the current job market. The class that started this is my most popular seminar/webinar: "Tips, Tricks, and

Strategy to be Found on LinkedIn." It has helped tens of thousands of people find their next job. I hope you will read this book and join those who have transitioned their career to the next opportunity.

With these strategies, you will spend more time answering recruiters' contacts than posting on job boards. This seminar/webinar helped job seekers get two to three inbound recruiter contacts a week when properly implemented.

It takes approximately 80 hours to put this strategy in place. There are no shortcuts to this implementation.

It is painful to hear people say that they have been in transition for many months and have made little progress in their job search.

I met with a friend who had paid for a costly job search package. It included a position resume, a LinkedIn profile, and extra job search collateral. Unfortunately, it did not work but looked pretty.

Unfortunately, he made very little progress in the last six months with his job search. Never-the less, he attended my Tips and Tricks webinar class.

Two weeks later, we had a follow-up coffee meeting, and he was knee-deep in interviews. So if you are not having success, this is the place to get moving in your job search.

Chapter 1
LinkedIn Background and Statistics

A job search today can be visualized as a three-legged stool:

The stool's first leg is a **job push strategy**, approximating 10%–20% of the job landings. Job push strategy is the most traditional part of the job search strategy. It is where the job seeker responds to job boards, job advertisements, contingent and retained recruiters. In addition, job seekers will research current open positions, contact, and work with recruiters. This part of the job search used to be about 50% of the job search landings. However, the competitive nature of contingent recruiting and retained recruiting has become less of the job search market.

The stool's second leg is the **job networking strategy**, approximating 30%–40% of job landings. Networking is a very successful method for landing mid-level to senior positions.

There are a couple of sides to a job networking strategy. The first part of a networking strategy is attending networking events to meet people from various industries to help you with contacts in your target companies. The second part is networking with people at your target company, using those contacts to find or create an open position at your target company. Finally, the third part uses LinkedIn or other social media platforms to connect with your target company's employees, then uses those contacts to find and land a position.

The stool's third leg is the **job pull strategy**, approximating 30%–40% of job landings. The job pull strategy utilizes social networking sites, such as LinkedIn or Facebook. Today, LinkedIn is the most advanced and highly used social networking platform for job searches. Other specialized social media platforms for job searching exist, but most have not reached the critical masses as LinkedIn has. Social networking sites are listings of people, capabilities, and attributes. Most of the tools that social networking sites have for job seekers are meant for the recruiter and not the job seeker. Therefore, the premise of this book is to prepare the job seeker's profile so that the recruiters can find it.

Ninety percent of recruiters will not look at your profile if you do not have the following:

- A photo that does not convert to a thumbnail for search results, the next chapter is all about your photo

- 500 first-level connections

- You must have your contact information in the "About" field

- Your resume not be copied straight into your LinkedIn profile

- A profile that is easily readable via mobile and desktop

- Listing and describing your significant achievements

- Statistics on your achievements

- A call to action

- A great elevator speech

- Appropriate Keywords for your position

- A consistent theme throughout your profile (Branding)

500 First-Level Connections

LinkedIn no longer penalizes you if you do not have 500 first-level connections. They now only require 50 first-level connections to have a complete or all-star profile. Recruiters believe that you're not serious about your LinkedIn profile if you don't have 500 first-level connections. Recruiters understand that not having 500 first-level connections will reduce your appearance in LinkedIn searches. As such, they believe they can immediately eliminate you as a potential job candidate.

Ranking high on a LinkedIn search has become much more competitive. Having 500 first-level connections worked well five years ago. Today, you need between 5,000 and 8,000 first-level connections to have the same level of success. The reduction in the number of first-level connections is the foundation of how LinkedIn makes money. The last statistics show that more than 50% of LinkedIn revenue comes from HR or Enterprise subscriptions. Therefore, the recruiters need you to have many connections. This keeps them from having very expensive HR or Enterprise LinkedIn subscriptions, over $1,000 per month.

You must have your contact information in the "About" field

Recruiters do not want to work hard to find your contact information. If a recruiter has an HR LinkedIn subscription, they have access to your contact information.

If the recruiter does not have an HR subscription and is not a 1st level connection to you, they will not access your contact information. I recommend that you put your contact information at the bottom of your "About" field and go into the security settings, visibility of your profile & network section. Click on the "Who can see or download your email address" and change the default to everyone. This way, everyone can see your contact information. It would be best to leave this in "everyone" mode while you are in a job search.

Do Not Paste Your Resume Into LinkedIn

Many LinkedIn members will cut and paste their resumes into their LinkedIn profiles. Most recruiters want to see more about you and about what you do. A resume gives the recruiters only the most basic details of your previous work history. LinkedIn is a social networking site, and recruiters expect you to talk more about yourself related to your position. They do not want just the Group of cold descriptors that are on your resume.

Resumes typically are searched via the Application Tracking Systems. They use a search system, much like Microsoft Word. It only takes a single search hit occurrence to positively affect the search algorithm and get you on the review hit list.

LinkedIn's search algorithm more closely emulates the Google algorithm rather than the Application Tracking System. The LinkedIn search algorithm is a points-based system. It cares how many points you get on a given search. It is a very different philosophy compared to an Application Tracking System.

94% Of Recruiters Use LinkedIn To Vet Candidates' Resumes

When a recruiter looks at your resume, you should have an active link to LinkedIn. They will undoubtedly compare what your resume says with what your LinkedIn profile says. Therefore, it is important not to contradict your resume with your LinkedIn profile content.

LinkedIn should be a superset of your resume(s). If you're writing a specific resume for a particular job opportunity, it cannot contradict what is in your LinkedIn profile. A recruiter wants to gain extra insights from your LinkedIn profile compared to what they read on your resume. The more insights you can provide a recruiter via your profile, the more comfortable they will submit you to a hiring manager. Recruiters believe candidates with positive details in their LinkedIn profiles are more qualified than those with just resumes.

Listing Skills Increases Profile Page Views By Thirteen Times

Listing your skills on LinkedIn is a little tricky. I tell my clients to use their keywords in the "Skills" section. You have to ensure that the skills you are using are keywords from the "Skills" pulldown box. If they are not in the pulldown box, you will not get search points for them.

Skills are separately searchable items that are part of the sales navigator and Enterprise/HR search. So if you don't have your keywords in the LinkedIn Skills search area, a recruiter can miss them if they are specifically looking for them in the Skills area. Many people claim that having others endorse your skills is a very meaningless endeavor. However, recruiters still take Skills into account if you have a significant number of endorsements. It's really up to you to find and use this section; it can be a huge help for most people in the job search. I tell people that everyone in the Group should be endorsing each member for all their skills—allowing them to get enough endorsements to be meaningful for the recruiter.

Unless you have 25 endorsements for each skill, it's just not fruitful to a recruiter. So reach out to your friends and get your skills endorsed. It shouldn't take you all that long, just a little bit of emailing and some dedication. Most people are more than willing to endorse your skills. There is more of an upside to getting endorsements than a downside, so I suggest you spend a little time getting this done. They will stay with you forever, so you merely have to do it once.

Many Firms Have Outsourced First And Second Level Research

Many firms have outsourced their first-level and second-level job-search research outside the US. These recruiters use LinkedIn as their sole pool of candidates for their research position for the most part. Most of these outsourced firms cannot use candidates' resumes. It is because most resumes have too much PII data (Personally Identifiable Information) in them. Most recruiting organizations do not believe it is good to have this information outside the United States. In addition, outsourced firms do not want to take responsibility for shipping resumes outside the United States and getting sued for having PII data released. So not only do they not send them resumes,

most of these researchers only utilize the Free
LinkedIn subscription. It causes problems with
their ability to see the entire LinkedIn member-
ship. As a result, many LinkedIn subscribers
put a word-based resume as an attachment to
their LinkedIn profile, with much of the PII
data removed.

One In Twenty LinkedIn Members Are Recruiters

Because one in 20 LinkedIn members are
recruiters, this gives most job seekers a large
pool of potential connections they can make.
Recruiters connect with recruiters, thereby
giving you more visibility to other recruiters.
Since most recruiters do not have HR or
Enterprise LinkedIn subscriptions, having
many first-level connections makes searching
easier. One of the big things I tell job seekers is
that recruiters are their buddies. Connect with
recruiters who recruit in your field of endeavor.
Since recruiters are the most likely to connect
with you, it gives you a large pool of folks to
become first-level connections. You can never
have enough first-level connections.

Seven Out Of Ten 18-to 35-year-old Professionals Find Their Jobs Via Social Media

Two years ago, this number was less than five out of ten who used social media as their primary source for their job search. It is expected that this evolution will continue and expand upward of 35-year-olds. You are beginning to see more senior job seekers getting their first contact from a LinkedIn source.

The traditional job search is changing in the market to allow for expediency. One of the reasons social media is working and accepted more and more often is that the traditional mechanism has become very costly. Many job descriptions for positions have been "dumbed down" for legal purposes. It allows companies more flexibility in their hiring. The more companies do this, the more they have to address more and more job applications before finding a suitable candidate.

Many companies recruiting above the most junior people see only one good resume out of 300 to 400 submissions. If you look at the math of what it costs to go through this many applicants, you'll find the number is staggering.

For example, if the HR manager is going to submit 20 job applicants to the hiring manager, that would mean that they have to go through at least 6,000 job applications.

If you do the math, it's 6,000 times five minutes to process each applicant via the Application Tracking System, which gives you 30,000 minutes. Then 30,000 minutes divided by 60 minutes per hour gives you 500 hours. So it breaks down to 12 to 13 weeks, depending on your workweek. It is why LinkedIn is becoming more popular every year.

LinkedIn Cheat Sheet

www.igniteyourLinkedInprofile.com/ cheat sheet

Chapter 2
Mesmerize The LinkedIn Recruiter With Your Picture!

A professional photo on LinkedIn is typically a headshot. Most recruiters believe that they can tell a lot about someone's personality by looking at their picture. Below you'll find a silly example of what not to do.

Six Poor Profile Photos:

Attributes of a Good Photo:

a. You do not necessarily need to use a professional photographer as long as you have a good camera or high-quality cell phone to take the picture.

b. You may want to use a mini flexible tripod to wrap around a pole or lampstand with a cell phone holder, even better, a full-size tripod. You can also use the many kinds of mini tripods and stand them on a bookcase shelf. There is generally a friend that has a tripod if you ask around.

c. If you have a good camera, you can take pictures in repeat mode, try different smiles and expressions, and pick the best. If you take your picture, I suggest that you test it on Photo-feeler, listed below.

d. The camera should be above the picture candidate's eye level to reduce the neck and face elongation. It is my problem with pictures; my wrinkly neck is ugly.

e. You can use a white or cream color bed sheet for a background. You may need to iron the sheet to get the wrinkles out. I recommend a lighter colored background to make the lighting easier. The best result is to stay at least four feet away from your photographic background. If you use a darker background, you need better lighting. It would be best to be further away from a dark background, or you may not have enough contrast between you and the background.

f. Regardless of the picture-taking device, you need to use portrait mode and reduce the depth of field. So the background is slightly out of focus or just fuzzy. You want you to stand out in the photo, not your background.

g. The subject should dress in the appropriate business attire for the position they are pursuing. Do not dress in the same color as the background. Your hair should not be the same color as the background. Your hair should be a contrasting color to the picture background.

h. The light for the picture should be coming from behind or to the side photographer. It will allow the subject's face to be well lit. Do not use strongly upward or downward pointing light or the face shadows will be elongated. Slightly upward-facing light is best at about 10 to 15 degrees off of horizontal to the face.

i. The picture of the candidate should be from the shoulders to the top of the head. The subject does not necessarily have to be in the exact center of the picture. It can be off to the side or slightly high, but it should be close to the center.

j. A high percentage of recruiters believe they can gain insights into the pictured candidate's personality. They try to read the facial expression of the subject. You must have a professional smile and a pleasant demeanor when you pose for your picture. It will give an excellent personal impression to the recruiter. There are online picture-review sites that can help you.

k. Many people say that natural light is better than artificial light when taking someone's photo. However, getting the right amount of natural light from the right direction is not always that simple. Good artificial light from a set of "daylight" light bulbs can be as good as natural light.

l. Do not try to take a "funny face" picture.

m. "LinkedIn Photo Guidelines" reserve the right to remove your photo if it is not a likeness of you or a headshot photo. For example, if you put an image of a company logo, landscape, animal, word, or phrase in the photo area, LinkedIn can remove it without notice.

n. The minimum dot pitch for a LinkedIn photo is 400 X 400 pixels. The maximum is 20,000 X 20,000 pixels. The photo must be in a PNG, JPG, or GIF format. I tell most people to use 400 X 400 pixels. If your picture is in the larger pixel size sometimes takes several minutes to render the thumbnail transformation of your profile photo.

o. You can use Microsoft Paint or Adobe Photoshop Elements to crop the picture and adjust the dot pitch.

p. iPhone uses HEIC extension. You need to convert it to JPG to use on LinkedIn. There are many free conversion sites on the Internet.

It may be helpful to have your profile reviewed by a photo review service such as Photofeeler. www.photofeeler.com

My Somewhat Good Picture That Needs To Be Done Over:

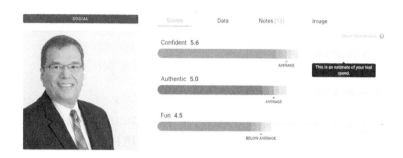

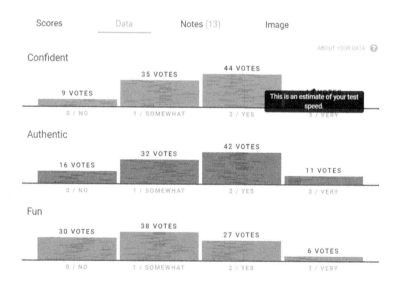

Scores	Data	Notes (13)	Image

"Smile seems a bit forced to me."

"Would prefer a different expression."

"Great photo!"

"Photo seems a bit artificial to me."

"Smile seems a bit forced to me."

"Great outfit!"

"Great photo!"

"Great smile!"

"Photo seems a bit artificial to me."

"Smile seems a bit forced to me. And teeth seem too white."

"Smile seems a bit forced to me."

"Smile seems a bit forced to me."

"Eyes seem over-edited."

This is an estimate of your test speed.

Three Good Profile Photos with Photofeeler reviews:

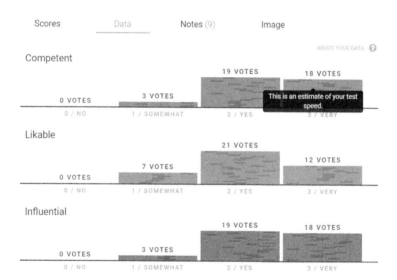

Scores   Data   Notes (9)   Image

"Great photo!"

"Great photo!"

"Photo seems professional to me."

"Great photo!"

"Great photo!"

"Would prefer a different expression."

"Great photo!"

"Photo seems professional to me."

"Great photo!"

Donald J Wittman • 43

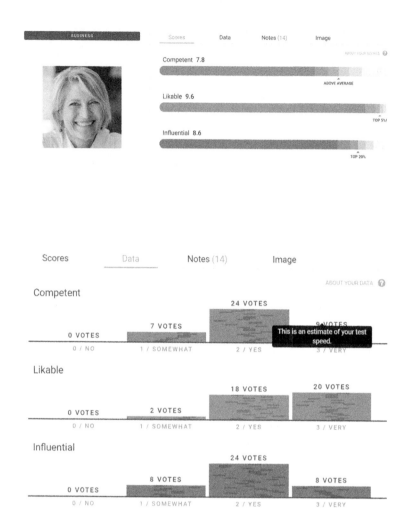

Scores   Data   Notes (14)   Image

"Great smile!"

"Seems a bit too close-up. Would prefer if it weren't cropped as tightly."

"Photo seems professional to me."

"Would prefer a different pose."

"Great photo!"

"Great smile!"

"Great smile!"

"Great photo!"

"Great photo!"

"I think they seem a bit young in this photo."

"Great smile!"

"Great smile!"

"Great photo!"

"Great photo!"

This is an estimate of your test speed.

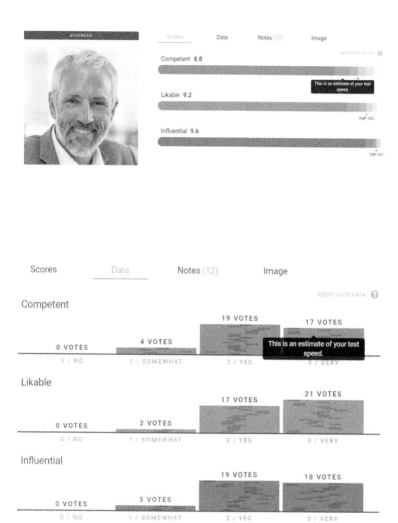

"Great photo!"

"Photo seems professional to me."

"Great photo!"

This is an estimate of your test speed.

"Photo seems professional to me."

"Photo seems professional to me."

"Great smile!"

"Photo seems professional to me."

"Photo seems professional to me."

"Hair is slightly too close in tone to backdrop. Shot unnecessarily crops out a segment of your right shoulder. The toothy smile risks coming off insincere. Advise smiling w/o showing teeth + slightly altering cropping and background color."

"Great photo!"

"Photo seems professional to me."

"exceptional smile, looking wise"

LinkedIn Search Thumbnail:

So let's talk about your thumbnail photo that shows up in a LinkedIn search, which is the first thing recruiters see when you show up in a search. Most recruiters will not choose your profile if your thumbnail photo is not showing up. There are two reasons this will happen. First, the picture is the wrong size or pitch. Second, LinkedIn is having trouble rendering it as a thumbnail, or you do not have a picture at all. Make sure your photo works appropriately. It is straightforward to test. All you have to do is a LinkedIn search that you know your profile should show up in and see if your thumbnail picture appears appropriately. If it's not, or it takes more than a few seconds to render, that means something is wrong. Please fix it quickly so that you are not passed over in searches in the future.

Nancy Nelson • 1st
CIO, COO
Greater New York City Area

Current: Resource Management Executive,

 360 shared connections

"The LinkedIn Guide to the Perfect #WorkSelfie"

Chapter 3
Branding Your LinkedIn Profile—Loretta Stevens

BRAND YOUR EDGE™ by Loretta Stevens, CEO and Brand Expert at Competitive Edge Branding.

Branding is essential in the selection of the keywords that you use in your headlines. You also use keywords in other high-value areas of your LinkedIn profile. If you do not add your main headline keywords in your other headlines, they may not be searchable. I only suggest using your title in your main headline if your search results for your title are not ranking in search. The main headline of your LinkedIn profile is the essential part of your profile. The next most important section is your current Experience/job position then, the following three previous job positions in your LinkedIn profile. Take great care to utilize them for your important keywords and job attributes. Also, be sure to brand yourself through your profile using your core values, strengths, and skills for relevancy, consistency, and validation of your "personal brand."

Your "personal brand" is a powerful tool and is the foundation to your LinkedIn success. Firstly, it is the *one unique factor* that proves how your expertise is different from others that you can quickly bring to your LinkedIn marketplace and use as your competitive edge. Second, having a clear, well thought out, written personal brand on your LinkedIn profile that also ranks well is how you will get the results that you desire from job hunting and attracting new clients. Finally, your "personal brand" profile combined with Don's "Ignite Your LinkedIn Profile" system is your pathway to winning results on LinkedIn.

This chapter will provide you with my Brand Your Edge ™ personal brand formula that is easy to complete and discover unique factors about yourself. You will then use the Brand Your Edge ™ formula as a framework to build a personal brand statement, profile summary, success stories, and videos for your LinkedIn brand. Finally, be sure to source and integrate the proper keywords that Don teaches you in

Ignite Your LinkedIn Profile, and you will have a nicely branded LinkedIn page.

After 15 years of delivering personal brand development for just about every profession and industry, also understanding and working through the challenges of how one "discovers" their "personal brand." I have condensed hundreds of brand discovery coaching hours into a fun exercise that has multiple uses. The best part is that the Brand Your Edge ™ formula takes about 15 minutes to complete.

The takeaway from my Brand Your Edge ™ formula is the technique that is used for discovery. In comparison, you may not land on the first try, your perfect power brand, from doing the exercise. Instead, you will learn the process for how to create, synthesize for yourself, build it out, and then leverage your results by creating stories that help you to stand out, attract the right audience, and open doors.

Through many workshops, training, and individual coaching sessions, discovering and building a personal brand and making it successful was confusing for many people for years. While the term "personal branding" became mainstream and was integrated into the coaching industry, many people still found it hard to get results.

Many self-assessment tools are available to help extract your top strengths, skills, talents, core values, personality, and more that help defines what makes one unique. However, what did not exist until now was a branding formula used to get to the core understanding of how to make a personal brand work for you professionally, which can also be used as a powerful marketing tool for your LinkedIn profile.

Before I get into the Brand Your Edge™ formula, I understand that completing the formula requires that you pull some data about yourself. You must *know Thyself* in 3 areas that include identifying your top strengths, skills, and core values to draw results. If you find that after you complete the Brand Your Edge™ formula that you are not ready for market with your results, you should invest in a few self-assessment tools and redo the Brand Your Edge™ formula to achieve better results.

OK, are you ready? We are going to be working in 3 columns. Please take out a piece of paper and position it landscape. At the top of the page, write The Brand Your Edge™ Formula. Make a column on the left side and write My Core Values. For starters, list your top 5 Core Values. Here is sample #1 to follow:

MY CORE VALUES

    1. DRIVE

    2. AUTHENTIC

    3. TRUST

    4. COLLABORATIVE

    5. FRIENDLY

Next, make a column to the right of the first column and list your top 5 strengths. Here is sample #2 to follow:

MY TOP STRENGTHS

1. **STRATEGIC**

2. **CRITICAL THINKER**

3. **CREATIVE**

4. **LEADERSHIP**

5. **FACILITATOR**

Then, make a third column to the right of My Top Strengths and list your top skills. Here is sample #3 to follow:

MY TOP SKILLS

1. **WEB DEVELOPER**

2. **PROBLEM SOLVER**

3. **COMMUNICATION**

4. **VIDEO MARKETING**

5. **TRAINER**

Now you should have three columns and your lists. Here is a sample of what your sheet of paper filled in should look like:

THE BRAND YOUR EDGE™ FORMULA

MY CORE VALUES	MY TOP STRENGTHS	MY TOP SKILLS
DRIVEN	STRATEGIC	WEB DEVELOPER
AUTHENTIC	CRITICAL THINKER+	PROBLEM SOLVER
TRUST (ED)	CREATIVE (ITY)	COMMUNICATION (OR)
COLLABORATIVE	LEADERSHIP	VIDEO MARKETING
FRIENDLY	FACILITATOR +	TRAINER

Next, start to connect the words into brand statements across each row to see how they fit. You may have to change the tense of the word so that it can turn into a powerful brand statement. You can also interchange the words from different rows so that they work best for your personal brand. In this sample set, we are using a list of 5 keywords under each column; however, there is no limit to the number of keywords that you can add that describe yourself under each column.

As the words come together and turn into statements, you may want to become more specific by adding an industry, target audience, or individuals you work with or would like to work with. Here are some samples to follow:

1. Driven, strategic, web developer *for startup manufacturing companies*

2. Authentic, critical thinker, and *excellent* problem solver *for global accounting firms*

3. Trusted, creative, communicator *for TV news channels*

4. Collaborative leader who creates video marketing *for insurance executives*

5. Friendly facilitator and corporate trainer *who transforms sales teams and top-line growth for software companies.*

As you can see, you can become creative in connecting your keywords into brand statements and even longer messages that help your reader become more explicit about who you are and the marketplace that you serve in a simple yet powerful way.

The Brand Your Edge™ formula can be used as a framework for developing stories from each of the statements that you created. More specifically, with modest effort, you can define 1-5 situations where each brand statement is true from a problem that you solved. You can also use the CAR analogy (*Challenge-Action-Result*) to help you create each story. I invite you to go deeper on each brand statement to find some gold in your background that you can use for your LinkedIn profile to stand out strategically. Use the Brand Your Edge™ formula more than once to learn more ways to communicate about yourself alongside IGNITE YOUR LINKEDIN PROFILE for your career and business marketing needs.

Loretta Stevens is an accomplished branding expert, executive transition coach, and CMOx for 7 figures at Competitive Edge Branding. Learn more about Loretta at www.LinkedIn .com/in/lorettaastevens and the Brand Your Edge™ Methodology and find an effective way to communicate your personal brand that fills the gap in your business and career at www.cebranding.com

Chapter 4
Functional Fit

Overview of Functional Fit

We raised the topic of Functional Fit in the Introduction. "Functional Fit" is important because it comes from the job requirements listed in the hiring position's job description. First, a recruiter will break down the high point requirements, which are keywords. Usually, a single job requirement is in a short sentence.

Keywords are the next level of specificity:

- Keyword strings are generally one to five words long. Most often, keywords are one to two terms. LinkedIn may not like keywords strings that are longer than two words. The longer the keyword string, the higher the likelihood it may not be searchable.

- Technology positions tend to have one to three-word keyword strings.

- Marketing positions tend to have one to five-word keyword strings; you need to try your best to shrink it down to a minimal number of terms.

- Some outlier positions have keyword strings up to seven words long. Long keyword strings may be better when you break them into two separate strings.

- Recruiters use these keywords to search for prospective job candidates. In general, recruiters will first try to use the fewest and most essential position keywords and add keywords to narrow down the search results.

Kforce is a nationwide recruiting firm that surveyed many recruiters. They first wanted to find out the size of the keyword search strings recruiters are using. Next, they tried to find the content of LinkedIn search strings recruiters are using. All this is to find prospective job candidates more reliably. Their results are below.

Kforce Keyword Statistics – search keywords:

- Minimum five keywords/keyword strings plus title

- Maximum 16 keywords/keyword strings plus title

- Average 12 keywords/keyword strings plus title

I have tested over a thousand clients' LinkedIn profiles. The job seeker's target "position title" testing has resulted in 80% not having their target "position title" rank in LinkedIn search on the first three pages in their target market.

Why is it important to rank in the first three pages? Look below at another Kforce survey. The average recruiter will not find you if the recruiter search does not show up on the first three pages (or the first 22 profile results).

Kforce Statistics search profile visited:

- Minimum eight profiles visited

- Maximum 50 profiles visited

- Average of 22 profiles visited

The testing I have conducted for "Position Keywords" is as problematic with job seekers as position title results. I asked the same clients for their top ten targets, "Position Keywords," to test them. Approximately 50% did not know or have ten "Position Keywords/Keyword Strings" identified.

Those that did have their target position keywords identified:

- less than 80% had more than four "Position Keywords" ranked on the first three pages in their target local job market,

- less than 20% had five to six keywords ranked on the first three pages in their target market,

- less than one percent had all ten ranked on the first three pages in their target local job market.

The statistics above demonstrate that you are unlikely to show up in the recruiter's average search if you do not show up on the first three pages.

What does all this mean? I try to get my clients to identify 20 keywords/keyword strings to help develop their search testing that will rank in searches.

In Chapter 8, we will do an overview of a process to find position keywords.

Recruiters will only visit enough LinkedIn profiles to meet the requirements of the position search. So let's say they have to find twenty potential job candidates that meet the provided job requirements. This is, by the way, more than average.

Let's assume that the search yields an 80% success rate; then, the recruiter will not go past page three (or 24 profiles). If we go so far as to say that there is only a 50% success rate, that is still only four LinkedIn search pages. So what does this mean if you are not on the first three pages of a position search? That means you are not going to be found by the recruiter or researcher.

LinkedIn Versus ATS Search

An ATS system (Applicant Tracking System) manages resumes and job applications. This application uses a Microsoft Word-like search functionality with partial fit results that provide maximum user inclusion. The ATS system typically uses a non-points-based result. Search results for the ATS system can be adjusted using various parameters to give more meaningful results. However, this is sometimes a hindrance and sometimes a blessing. Sometimes it is called fuzzy logic results.

LinkedIn provides exact-fit point-based probabilistic search results. LinkedIn search results offer a Boolean search capability; someone cannot manipulate for fuzzy logic results. LinkedIn only understands exact matches. LinkedIn has dabbled with title adaption, such as VP for Vice President, but results were inconsistent.

Chapter 5
LinkedIn Profile Checklist

Your LinkedIn Profile Must Be 100% Complete

If your profile is not 100% complete, you will see a box that looks like the one below. This Profile Strength box tells you the strength which LinkedIn has broken down into five levels:

1. Beginner

2. Intermediate

3. Advanced

4. Expert

5. All-Star

Which university or school did you attend?
Add your school so that classmates and alumni can easily find you

If you click on the next button shown above, LinkedIn with walk you through what is missing. This feature has been brought back and is very helpful to most beginners and those trying to use the help files, which tend to be confusing.

Your Dashboard
Private to you
☆ All Star

987	295	569
Who viewed your profile	Post views	Search appearances

What do you need to get to an "All-Star" profile strength?

Your LinkedIn profile needs to be 100% complete to rank best in a search. This means you should have an All-Star LinkedIn profile. Your profile strength shows up on your LinkedIn Dashboard on the upper right-hand side, as shown below.

I am not going to cover what you need for each level of profile strength. Instead, I am just going to cover the "All-Star" profile level of power.

    A. Profile picture

    B. Industry

    C. Location

    D. About field (three complete lines, some say 200 to 500 characters)

    E. Experience (current position plus two previous job positions)

    F. Skills (five skills or more)

    G. Education

    H. Connections (need at least 50 LinkedIn 1st level connections)

You Are No Longer Required To Have Recommendations

It would be best to be careful with recommendations because they are considered part of your LinkedIn profile search text. If you have too many LinkedIn recommendations or the recommendations are long, this can impact search results. In addition, the amount of additional text can work against you in LinkedIn searches. This is because LinkedIn search works on keyword density; the more text you have, the more keywords you need to rank. We will talk more about what makes up this problem later in the book.

Use LinkedIn Locations

You should use LinkedIn locations rather than the city you live in, the first graphic below. LinkedIn has broken the mapping between the city and LinkedIn locations almost every year. When LinkedIn makes updates to their LinkedIn search algorithm, LinkedIn locations generally break. If your "city" and the mapping of "city" to "LinkedIn Locations" is broken, you will not show up in recruiter searches. Most recruiters use LinkedIn locations in their job candidate searches, shown in the second graphic below.

Country/Region *

| United States | ▼ |

ZIP code

| 06877 |

Locations within this area

| Ridgefield, Connecticut | ▼ |

Country/Region *

| United States | ▼ |

ZIP code

| 06877 |

Locations within this area

| Greater New York City Area | ▼ |

I had quite a few clients not showing up in a LinkedIn search for up to two months when LinkedIn locations mapping was having difficulties. You can see the use of LinkedIn locations (Greater New York City Area) below with Nancy's profile.

Nancy Nelson • 1st

CIO, COO

Greater New York City Area

Current: Resource Management Executive,

 377 shared connections

Your Default LinkedIn Headline

Your LinkedIn headline is the first thing that recruiters will see when they choose to view your profile. LinkedIn defaults to merging your title and company name from your current position in your first experience area. Therefore, position titles are the wrong thing to have in your main headline. When someone searches for your current job position, they are exploring the headline of your current position, not your LinkedIn profile's primary headline. Recruiters will know if you do not customize your main headline.

Your LinkedIn Profile Needs A Great Headline

Your main headline should tell the recruiter what your "High Value" skills are, what you are an expert at, and what made you succeed. The first one hundred characters or so of the main headline show up in your search results; make it count.

A few examples of the 220 character headlines with the search results:

Human Resources, HR Business Partner | Employee Relations | HR Compliance | HR Governance | HR Change Management | Talent Management | Performance Management | HR Transformation | Training | HR Director | HR Leader

Craig E. Cunningham, SPHR, HRBP, VP, HR Director · 1st in
Human Resources, HR Business Partner | Employee Relations | HR Com...
New York City Metropolitan Area

Digitalization Strategies | Strategic Automation | Internet Innovation | Digital Technology | Digital Strategy | Digital Transformation | Technology Leadership | Digital Consulting | Agile Marketing | Change Management

Montgomery (Monty) Mars, CMO, CTO, Strategy · 1st
Digitalization Strategies | Strategic Automation | Internet Innovation | D...
New York City Metropolitan Area

Operating Partner, Board of Directors, New Business Development, Digital Strategy, Social Media Marketing, Strategic Planning, Marketing Strategy, Corporate Development, Online Marketing, Strategic Partnerships, CMO, CEO

Thomas G. Taber, CEO, CMO, CRO, BOD, Investor · 2nd
Operating Partner, Board of Directors, New Business Development, Digital Strategy, Social Medi...
Danbury, CT

Experienced Corporate Board Director, Vice-Chair, Chair Compensation Committee, Nominating Governance Committee, Marketing Committee, Audit Committee, Communications Committee, HR Committee, Board Development Committee

Nancy Nelson, · 2nd
Experienced Corporate Board Director, Vice Chair, Chair Compensation Committee, Nominatin...
New York City Metropolitan Area

Great headlines are written in two different forms or a combination of both:

- The first and simplest uses individual keywords, keyword pairs, or keyword triplets separated by vertical bars or commas.

- The second is by a complex sentence or a combination of both.

- For those who have an excellent marketing knack, the complex sentence is what I prefer. The main headline character length increased from 150 characters to 220 characters, including spaces.

A few examples of the old 150 character length headline are below:

Blockchain Expert | Digital Marketing and Branding Expert | ICO Marketing | Social Media Strategist

Safety Personnel | Administrative Support | Client Relations | Project Manager | Customer Service

Award-Winning Design Leader Who Engineers and Implements Next-Generation Solutions and Results-Driven Initiatives

A few examples of a branded 220 character headline:

Example 1: Craig's branded headline.

Your HR Business Partner and Recruitment Partner, Employee Relations, HR Compliance, HR Governance, HR Change Management, Talent Management, Performance Management, HR Transformation, HR Director, HR Leader Human Resources

Example 2: Monty's branded headline

Comprehensive and Diverse Technology Thought Leader, Digitalization Strategies, Strategic Automation, Internet Innovation, Digital Technology Digital Strategy, Digital Transformation, Technology Leadership, Digital Consulting, Agile Marketing

Example 3: Thomas's branded headline

Driver of Innovation, Performance, and Growth, Operating Partner, Board of Directors, New Business Development, Digital Strategy, Social Media Marketing, Strategic Planning, Marketing Strategy, Online Marketing, Strategic Partnerships

Example 4: Nancy's branded headline

Leading Corporate Board Structures and Committees, Experienced Corporate Board Director, Vice-Chair, Chair Compensation Committee, Nominating Governance, Marketing Committee, Audit Committee, HR Committee, Board Development

---

Branding your LinkedIn profile headline is essential in selecting the keywords you use in your headlines. You also use keywords in other high-value areas of your LinkedIn profile. If you do not put your main headline keywords in your other headlines, they may not be searchable.

I only suggest using your title in your main headline if your search results for your title are not ranking in search. The main headline of your LinkedIn profile is the essential part of your profile.

The next most important section is your current Experience/job position, the following three previous job positions of your LinkedIn profile. Take great care to utilize them for your important keywords and job attributes.

A Powerful LinkedIn About Field

Your LinkedIn "About" field is your marketing pitch. Please make sure your "About" field does not read like a resume. You want it to be personable, you want to use friendly language, and you want to show a bit of yourself. Most recruiters hate it when people put resumes speak in their LinkedIn "About" field. So instead, your About field should answer the question: Why should I hire you?

Your LinkedIn About field is the most potent part of your LinkedIn profile from a recruiter's perspective. It tells the recruiter what you have done and what you can do for them.

Your "About" field is an opening statement about who you are and what makes you successful. The first three to five lines of your "About" field are your "About" field's best real estate. This area of the "About" field is sometimes referred to as your elevator speech.

The center area of your "About" field is where I recommend including three examples of your major successes. First, you should tell your story, such as what made you successful and what achievements you had. Second, I recommend using the STAR, CAR, or SOAR format for listing your accomplishments. I hear over and over again from executive recruiters that there is not enough good information. So feed the recruiter what they want, a great elevator speech to start, three great examples of achievements with stats (Stats with make or break your "About" field and call to action in your contact me statement.

For example:
HIGHLY AVAILABLE SYSTEMS

One of our companies biggest challenges was to address the uptime availability of the Company's website.

Using a group of five highly available systems enhancements, we were able to get our production websites to 99.99% availability.

This project brought the Company the equivalent of 13 extra business days of demand generation the following year.

Have Your Contact Information In Your About Field

At the end of your "About" field, you should put a CTA (call to action) in the closing statement to get the recruiters to contact you about a potential position. Your contact information should follow immediately. See below my call to action:

CONTACT ME

I'd welcome the opportunity to schedule a time to talk about your LinkedIn challenges and explore how we may be able to work together. I teach seminars and workshops and provide one-on-one tutoring and coaching to clients looking to strengthen their LinkedIn presence.

I can be reached at:
Email: don@don.com
Telephone: 333-444-555

One of the big problems we discuss later is that only about one-third of recruiters have the Enterprise or HR LinkedIn subscription. This subscription allows them to see everyone on LinkedIn, along with their contact information. So for the remaining recruiters who do not have these expensive subscriptions and are not the first-level connection to you, you need to have your contact information in your "About" field.

Your LinkedIn Profile Must Be In Sync With Your Resume

You must maintain your LinkedIn profile such that it is in sync with the resumes you send out. As I mentioned before, 90+% of recruiters will validate your resume against your LinkedIn profile. Therefore, it is a necessity to make sure that your resume does not contradict your LinkedIn profile. Most recruiters will reject an applicant if this is the case.

Have Statistics Tell Your Story

You should have statistics about your successes in your current experience position and previous experience positions in your profile to support your About field statements. Even if the Company you work for does not allow you to use the statistics directly, it is possible to obfuscate them enough to not company confidential information. Recruiters are looking for statistics in your profile to amplify your successes and what they can potentially expect of you in the future, so please don't overlook this item.

Some examples:

- Dollars saved

- Dollar sales increase

- Percent better

- Percent increase

- Percent productivity increase

- Productivity improvement

- Time-to-market improvement

- Workforce savings

- Supply chain improvements

- Tax savings

- Agility improvements

- Capital savings

- Expense reduction

Extension To Your Name Line

LinkedIn is now allowing you to put certifications and degrees at the end of your name line. To be clear, LinkedIn still says in your user agreement that you should not use it for anything but your name. However, LinkedIn has not been enforcing this rule. This area is a high-point LinkedIn area, so it is a valuable area to put your keywords.

You must maintain your first name and initials in the first box and your last name at the beginning of the second box. After your name, you can put degrees or certifications, but be careful not to put in too much. Sometimes this will cause your "name" to no longer be searchable. You should not put your first and last name in the first name box and fill your last name box with titles and certifications. There is a high probability that a recruiter or anyone will not be able to find your profile by a name search in the standard search box. If the person doing the searching has a paid LinkedIn subscription, they have more ways to search, which makes this less of an issue. However, approximately 50% do not have a paid subscription, so it's best not to overuse these fields. You can see the examples below.

Standard Name Field Usage:

Standard Name Field Usage With Certifications And Degrees

Do Not Do This With The Standard Name Field

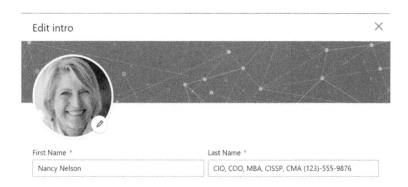

Edit intro   ✕

First Name *

Nancy Nelson

Last Name *

CIO, COO, MBA, CISSP, CMA (123)-555-9876

Chapter 6
Punctuation, Readability, And Fonts

Your LinkedIn Profile Must Be Easy To Read

Your LinkedIn profile's readability is critical to the first and second levels of recruiters. There are two factors in readability. So this means the first factor is white space, so the text is not just a big blob. The average first-and second-level recruiters are sometimes called *researchers*. They typically only have to read your About field and experience headlines. If there is not enough white space in your About field to break up the text, it is challenging to read physically. The second factor is sentence complexity. It is considered best to write your profile at an eighth-grade level or lower. If you don't have a tool to do this, keeping sentences smaller than 18 words will help.

The typical first-level and second-level recruiters have small screens on their computers.

LinkedIn has changed the font color from black to gray, making it more challenging to stand out on a small screen. LinkedIn claims it is easier on the eyes. Some research reinforces this, but my experience (and complaints from others) contradicts this.

If you're someone (like a recruiter) who reads resumes and LinkedIn profiles a large part of their day, gray is more taxing on their eyes than black. So be kind to the first and second level of recruiters and make it more readable. We will talk about some examples of this later on.

The other problem with your profile not being comfortable to read is when it is read on a mobile phone, it may look like a blob of text on a phone screen. So be aware of this, and we will see some examples later of what to do to make it a little more readable.

Your Profile Must Have Plenty Of White Space

Your LinkedIn profile must be easy to read. You should not have more than seven lines without a line break. I prefer to make most paragraphs in my About field no more than three or four lines. Unfortunately, it is sometimes impossible to do this. A seven-line section in your About field on a typical PC ends up being a 20-line blob of text on your mobile phone. 60+% of all profile views on LinkedIn is viewed on a mobile device. If you don't make your LinkedIn profile easy to view on a desktop, it won't be enjoyable to read on a mobile device. See the examples below.

Example Of A Good About Field Via Desktop:

If your LINKEDIN PROFILE was on PAGE 1 for your JOB SEARCH or BUSINESS, what kind of success would that bring to the table? LinkedIn is the best place for business people to find other business people.

As a previous CTO, I combine in-depth technology expertise toward the use of LinkedIn. I have a set of processes to get my clients found. For those DIY'ers, I offer a variety of Training Classes and Webinars to help you understand my proven process.

HIGH CHALLENGE JOB SEARCH

The most common complaint, after professionals complete their LinkedIn Profiles, is Head Hunters are not finding them on LinkedIn.

I help Professionals find the right "KEYWORDS" for the position they aspire to and place these words in my client's profile for the best search results.

This is only one of five metrics that are important to LinkedIn Search. This process results in significantly

Example Of A Good About Field On A Mobile Phone:

If your LINKEDIN PROFILE was on PAGE 1 for your JOB SEARCH or BUSINESS, what kind of success would that bring to the table? LinkedIn is the best place for business people to find other business people.

As a previous CTO, I combine in-depth technical expertise toward the use of LinkedIn. I have a set of processes to get my clients found. For those DIY'ers, I offer a variety of Training Classes and Webinars to help you understand my proven process.

HIGH CHALLENGE JOB SEARCH

The most common complaint, after professionals complete their LinkedIn Profiles, is Head Hunters are not finding them on LinkedIn.

I help Professionals find the right "KEYWORDS" for the position they aspire to and place these words in my client's profile for the best search results.

This is only one of five metrics that are important to LinkedIn Search. This process results in significantly higher profile views and inbound contact rate.

Home   My Network   Post   Notifications   Jobs

Example 2 Of A Good About Field Via Desktop:

About

CHANGE LEADERSHIP, TRANSFORMATION: CREATES VALUE BY MAKING THE RIGHT MOVES

William believes growing business value is a lot like playing chess. "It's about adapting your game to how your customer reacts and moving your assets to the right places." Jon has made the right moves as a strategic President, innovator, and business builder for world class brands including AIG, American Express, Priceline, Microsoft and McKinsey JV's.

Bill thrives in organizations where he manages change and grows complex businesses. He is a marketing and metrics-driven leader with an entrepreneurial drive that "makes it happen" through market focus, innovative thinking, agile execution and collaborative teams. At AIG, he took an idea from concept to reality and created a $2 billion business.

VALUES COLLABORATION AND THOUGHT DIVERSITY

For Bill, a key trait of a transformation GM leader is the ability to get input from all sources and synthesize feedback to inform decisions. He interjects fun and humor to boost productivity. His collaborative style promotes what he calls "thought diversity." For him, that's a key to implementing innovation.

LEADS EBITDA GROWTH AS GM PRESIDENT

Bill exceeds EBITDA, revenue, and new customer targets. At AIG, his team delivered $280 million in EBITDA and 9 million new customers. Jon parlayed his classically trained experience into the digital age to grow disruptive businesses leveraging marketing, analytics and market trends. He was awarded two US patents: "Retaining Customers" and "Using Telesales Techniques."

Example 2 Of A Good About Field On A Mobile Phone:

 🔒 linkedin.com/mwlite/in [1] ⋮

If your LINKEDIN PROFILE was on PAGE 1 for your JOB SEARCH or BUSINESS, what kind of success would that bring to the table? LinkedIn is the best place for business people to find other business people.

As a previous CTO, I combine in-depth technical expertise toward the use of LinkedIn. I have a set of processes to get my clients found. For those DIY'ers, I offer a variety of Training Classes and Webinars to help you understand my proven process.

HIGH CHALLENGE JOB SEARCH

The most common complaint, after professionals complete their LinkedIn Profiles, is Head Hunters are not finding them on LinkedIn.

I help Professionals find the right "KEYWORDS" for the position they aspire to and place these words in my client's profile for the best search results.

This is only one of five metrics that are important to LinkedIn Search. This process results in significantly higher profile views and inbound contact rate.

Home   My Network   Post   Notifications   Jobs

Example Of A Bad About Field On A Desktop:

How do you choose a franchise with 4000+ brands in the market today? I consult with corporate professionals and new entrepreneurs to determine if business ownership is the best next chapter for you! Work feels quite different when your talent and time is invested in a business that's your own. As a multi-brand franchise owner myself, I am uniquely qualified to guide you through a process designed to sort through the clutter, dispel the myths and uncover the meaningful data points in choosing the best franchise for you while minimizing your risk.

>> Understand You First

Before pinpointing the best franchises opportunities that fulfill your lifestyle and financial goals, career aspirations and leverage your skills and talents, I get to know you first.

>> Develop Your Strategy

We take it all into consideration - your preferred geography, your family situation, your desired role in the

business, your comfort level for financing and your timeline.

>> Identify the Best Opportunities

Example Of A Bad About Field On A Mobile Phone:

How do you choose a franchise with 4000+ brands in the market today? I consult with corporate professionals and new entrepreneurs to determine if business ownership is the best next chapter for you!
Work feels quite different when your talent and time is invested in a business that's your own.
As a multi-brand franchise owner myself, I am uniquely qualified to guide you through a process designed to sort through the clutter, dispel the myths and uncover the meaningful data points in choosing the best franchise for you while minimizing your risk.
>> Understand You First
Before pinpointing the best franchises opportunities that fulfill your lifestyle and financial goals, career
aspirations and leverage your skills and talents, I get to know you first.
>> Develop Your Strategy
We take it all into consideration - your preferred geography, your family situation, your desired role in the
business, your comfort level for financing and your timeline.
>> Identify the Best Opportunities

Limit Boolean Operators, Punctuation, And Custom Fonts

There are two main reasons to limit Boolean operators in your LinkedIn profile. The first we talked about earlier, some of LinkedIn Boolean operators are also punctuation. LinkedIn has issues with parsing punctuation correctly. LinkedIn has some problems in search of punctuation other than the use of periods and commas.

If you have a keyword phrase such as "network technology:" in many cases, the search for "network technology" will fail. Because after technology, the ":" has become part of the word "technology." This is true of much of the standard punctuation we use. There is no documentation on this anywhere that I can find. When doing testing on clients' profiles, this is the case most of the time. I should say that this is not always the case, but it happens often enough to take note of. I take precautions to leave a space on both sides of most punctuation. There are some exceptions, such as "M&A" and "P&L," which work correctly.

First, I recommend my clients use spaces between most punctuation other than periods and commas. Second, it is a lot of work to test keywords in your LinkedIn profile. It is easier to assume this is always the case rather than spending hours validating if keywords are correctly resolving in a LinkedIn search.

Second, it is a good idea to limit Boolean operators in your LinkedIn profile for both Google and LinkedIn. It is not unusual for both search engines to get confused with embedded Boolean operators in the LinkedIn profile text. I agree that the problem is not consistent, but it often happens to take care of when using them. The Google Boolean operators are: &, /,-,(,). And LinkedIn Boolean operators are:-, (,), NOT, OR, AND. LinkedIn does not officially tell you to limit these; however, they sometimes cause problems in advanced searches. This is especially true when you're doing complex advance searches. I have had difficulties with having Boolean operators in the body of the profile.

Use Of Custom Fonts

LinkedIn now allows you to apply to job postings with your LinkedIn profile and attached resume. Many LinkedIn profiles use fancy bullets in the text of the "About and

Experience" area. They may also add fancy lightning bolts with or without color. This is not a good idea since most Application Tracking Systems that interface with LinkedIn do not like non-standard fonts. If you want to submit a job application via your LinkedIn profile, you should stick to standard fonts like Times New Roman, Arial, and Calibri. Why am I even talking about this? Many times, Application Tracking Systems do not support complex fonts. So what happens to your rejected application submission? Rejected job applications go to the ATS manual queue. Most companies do not try to recover rejected job application submissions, so they are in the bit bucket.

Some examples of arrows, pointers, and symbols to stay away from:

■ ◆ ◆ ● ❀ ✿ ◇ ▫ ━ ▫ ╔ ★ ☆ ✱ ❋ ✳ ✪ ✫ ✩ ✚ ✜ ☞
◄ ◄ ◄ ☞ ☜ ⇨ ▶ ◀ ▶ » ▲ ▼ ⇒ ⇓ ⇔ ⇕ ↘ ↗ ↘ ✎ ⇐ ⇛--
▶ 👗 🎁 👕 🥣 👜 👝 👞 👟 🥾 👢 💎 🕶

Having your resume on LinkedIn is a great way to help recruiters and can be used for job submission. LinkedIn did not support Microsoft "doc" or "docx" formats a couple of years ago. So many LinkedIn members started to use PDF formatted resumes. PDF resumes are problematic because only a tiny number of Application Tracking Systems support PDF documents. In addition, some PDF converters use features not generically supported. The result is many times; these PDF resumes end up in the bit bucket as well. When I was looking for a job, I was constantly reminded by recruiters and headhunters that I needed to submit my resume in Microsoft Word document format.

Below is an example of resume competencies:

These competencies should also be in your LinkedIn profile in this form or another. For example, if you list something in your resume, you need to list it in your LinkedIn profile.

Technology and Business Acumen that Optimize Business Results:

- *eCommerce*

- *Automated Quality Process*

- *IT Infrastructure/Telecom/Mobility*

- *Enterprise Turnarounds*

- *Enterprise Security and Compliance*

- *Business Growth Software Development*

- *Datacenter Optimization*

- *Profitability Enhancements*

- *Post-Acquisition System Managers*

- *Governance/Process Improvement*

- *Vendor Sourcing and Negotiations*

- *Team Leadership and Developments*

Below is an example of a resume overview:

These overview items should also be in your LinkedIn profile in this form or another. If you have it in your resume, you need to have it in your LinkedIn profile.

Global, results-driven IT Executive whose technical expertise and business acumen deliver accelerated enterprise-wide solutions on time and under budget. Optimizes business results through the organization, elimination of bureaucracy, innovation, and collaboration. Builds high-performing teams and develops them to deliver technically superior products and solutions with exceptional customer value. They are sought after as knowledge leader on business continuance and security. Navigates with expertise through key business life cycle inflection points, including critical mergers and acquisitions, organic growth, liquidity events, and turnarounds. They are solving the previously unsolvable.

Change Your Default Public URL

Most people consider it a poor style to use the automatically generated LinkedIn personal

URL. You should change your default public URL to a personalized URL. My public URL is http://www.LinkedIn.com/in/donaldjwittman. Not changing your default LinkedIn public URL leads people to believe that you are not familiar with the Internet. It demonstrates a lack of knowledge of technology. There are two places to change your public URL. The first place is on your profile page. The second is in your settings. Below are screenshots of each.

Screenshot Of Your Profile Page

Screenshot Of First Settings Page

Account	Privacy	Ads

How others see your profile and network information

How others see your LinkedIn activity

How LinkedIn uses your data

Job seeking preferences

Blocking and hiding

How others see your profile and network

Edit your public profile

Choose how your profile appears to non-logged in members via search engines or permitted services

Who can see your email address

Choose who can see your email address on your profile

Who can see your connections

Screenshot Of Edit Public Profile Page

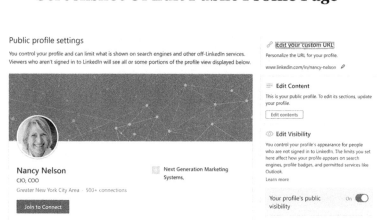

Public profile settings

You control your profile and can limit what is shown on search engines and other off-LinkedIn services. Viewers who aren't signed in to LinkedIn will see all or some portions of the profile view displayed below.

Nancy Nelson
CIO, COO
Greater New York City Area · 500+ connections

Join to Connect

Next Generation Marketing Systems,

✎ Edit your custom URL
Personalize the URL for your profile.
www.linkedin.com/in/nancy-nelson ✎

Edit Content
This is your public profile. To edit its sections, update your profile.
Edit contents

Edit Visibility
You control your profile's appearance for people who are not signed in to LinkedIn. The limits you set here affect how your profile appears on search engines, profile badges, and permitted services like Outlook.
Learn more

Your profile's public visibility   On ●

Chapter 7
What Affects LinkedIn Search Results

Your LinkedIn profile is ranked by:

- Keywords

- User activity

- User connections

- The number of endorsements you give

- The number of profile page views

- The number of postings

- The number of groups

- The number of endorsements you receive

User activity can help drive profile pages:

- Number of endorsements you give

- Number of level one connections you made

- Number of postings you made

- Number of groups you joined

- The number of recommendations you give

The Number One Thing In Search Is Keywords

(Functional Fit)

Let's assume the person who is searching for a great job candidate can see your LinkedIn profile. The next most important thing to your ranking is your keywords. There are two ways keywords are used in LinkedIn searches. The first is keyword density, and the second is keyword frequency. I know this seems pretty foolish, but the LinkedIn profile search is a points-based system. So the longer your LinkedIn profile is, the more frequently you have to put your keywords in your LinkedIn profile to rank in the search. That is why we also talk about keyword density.

Keyword density is the relationship of the amount of text in your profile, including recommendations, to the number of keywords in these areas, titles of your media, titles of attachments, projects, and other areas of your profile. So if you have a 10,000-word LinkedIn profile and you get 100 points in your search words, you have a relationship of one to 100. If you have a 5,000-word LinkedIn profile and you have 100 points, your search words have a relationship of one to 50. The better this relationship, the higher you will rank.

There are two methods to get your keywords to rank:

- Minimalist profile method

- Points-based profile method

The minimalist LinkedIn profile method is relatively simple. It works best for subject matter experts, consultants, and independent professionals. Start out your profile in the same way. You have your professional picture, your name line, your main headline, and your About field. The About field is very focused—start with standard stuff; the first couple of lines make you stand out. Then, important things like keywords. It is typically half the length of a typical About field (which is normally 2,000 characters).

The significant change is in your current position, and the following three positions need to be filled out, along with your company name. Typically, there are no recommendations to detract from the keyword density. You still have your skills and limited education information. The idea of taking these steps is to get an "All-Star" profile ranking from LinkedIn while leaving out as much low information text as possible.

A points-based LinkedIn profile typically has a well-populated About field and at least four positions in the profile. There is much more detail in the experience areas than in a minimalist profile. Most of these profiles include some recommendations, complete education, and other optional areas, which tends to make profiles long and use a large number of words. The more words in the profile you have, the more you have to repeat the occurrence of keywords for your position to rank well in searches.

The Next Big Thing That Helps Your Rank Is Page Views

If you compare the same profile under two different names, different emails, and different company names (while everything else remains the same).

The first candidate has:

- 8,000 LinkedIn first-level connections

- Ranking in the top 3% viewed within his connections

- 900 page views per 90 days

The second candidate has:

- 2,700 first-level connections

- Ranking in the top 14% viewed within his connections

- 400 pages views per 90 days

So what do you think the difference in search ranking for position title with five keywords in the US for all connection levels is? Not what you would expect.

The first candidate was on page one—Yea!

The second candidate was on page 45, basically lost in the dark depths of LinkedIn—Boo Hoo!

What Are Recruiters Looking For?

- A recruiter will first build a "keywords requirements" list and a potential "nice to have" requirements list.

- Having many first-level and Group connections makes your LinkedIn profile more likely to be found by a keyword search.

- LinkedIn is a social media site, so recruiters expect your profile to be more social and have insights about who you are.

Keywords Drive Page Views

- How many profile page views per 90 days do you get?

- It is commonly quoted that you need 1,000 profile page views for your first offer on LinkedIn.

At five profile page views per week, it takes 200 weeks to get 1,000 profile page views.

At ten profile page views per week, it takes 100 weeks to get 1,000 profile page views.

At 25 profile page views per week, it takes 40 weeks to get 1,000 profile page views.

At 50 profile page views per week, it takes 20 weeks to get 1,000 profile page views.

At 100 profile page views per week, it takes ten weeks to get 1,000 profile page views.

Chapter 8
Find Your Keywords

A good friend in a high-level HR role and his team could not find a viable candidate for a critical position for more than two years. He asked for my help finding potential candidates because the senior executives were getting upset (I am kind here) that their projects were not progressing as originally planned.

I sat down with my friend and his departmental recruiter and went over the job requirements and the formal job description document. The first problem was the published job requirements read as if the position was for an IT person, not a marketing person. In addition, the agile requirements were not precise, and their experience level was not evident.

In about two hours, we had a good set of job requirements. Within an hour, I presented them a list of 25 potential candidates within a 25-mile radius and in their industry. The takeaway is that job requirements need to be clear in the job description to recruit top candidates successfully. That is why I stress that you need to find excellent and written job descriptions with actual job requirements.

Finding Keywords For Your LinkedIn Profile

Finding keywords is a pretty straightforward mechanical process. Depending on your career level, you want five to 20 job descriptions that fit your job goal and fit your experience. For example, a junior-level programmer, marketer, financial, or HR professional should use five to ten job descriptions. A mid-level professional to a director-level programmer, marketer, financial, or HR professional should use ten to 15 job descriptions. Senior-level professionals should use 15 to 20 job descriptions.

It is imperative to find job descriptions for a position that you're looking for and make sure that you can execute the duties for the role properly. You should also take into account which industry you are considering as well. Keywords may differ by industry and may not work well across the board.

The more specific you can find a perfect fit for job descriptions, the better it will work.

Recruiters do not want someone who says they can do everything regardless of the industry. Recruiters have a position description and industry fit, and many of the job requirements can be industry-specific. One of the better places to find job descriptions is www.indeed. com.

You need to make sure that the job descriptions you choose have job requirements in them. I would stay away from job descriptions similar to what McKinsey puts out. The McKinsey job descriptions are generally five pages long and have minimal requirements information in them. Many of the job descriptions read like a lot of hot air, but to be fair, many companies are starting to follow this style. Three years ago, 90% of the job descriptions were well detailed with many primary and secondary job requirements; now, it seems to have moved down to 70%.

Recruiters are ditching poor job descriptions and using their own internally developed job requirement lists for the positions they are doing searches for. In addition, they are doing their research due to the ongoing obfuscation of the actual job requirements along with the client-provided job description and job requirements documents. The non-specific job descriptions give hiring managers more flexibility in hiring candidates.

Once you find the job descriptions that fit your ideal job, you cut and paste them into a single Word document. Then you edit out all the company profile information, education requirements, and things that you can control; HR disclaimers, legal disclaimers. Leave only the job requirements. There are two types; the ones required for the position and those that are nice to have. It would be best if you used both sets of job requirements in your keyword discovery process.

Once you remove all of the non-job-requirement information from your Word document, you then cut and paste the document into a word cloud such as www.wordle.net. Most of the word cloud products require JAVA. Make sure your browser can handle JAVA or find one that does not require it. There are many word cloud programs—it may take some time to search or find one, but they are out there.

I found the two edited job descriptions on Indeed.com. Some information is changed to protect the Company posting the position. These are not current positions. The yellow highlighted text should be removed because it will not help with keywords. In addition, the underlined text needs to be fixed because LinkedIn does not understand the meaning of "and." The repaired text will be in parenthesis.

First Example of Edited Job Descriptions:

Some Company is seeking a Chief Technology Officer who embodies our company core values listed above. This is a unique opportunity for a person possessing the right depth of talent, leadership, experience, passion, and drive. Reporting to the CEO, you'll be located with our executive staff at our global headquarters in Irvine, CA. Some Company hosts a large and complex online gaming environment and it is critical for this person to understand the dynamics associated with delivering products in this type of environment and then develop and implement strategic solutions.

Some Company attracts people who are bright, ambitious and confident, with an extremely strong desire to win. The successful candidate will be smart, candid, direct and non-political, with a highly developed sense of ethics, energy, confidence, creativity, and ambition. This person will be team-oriented, with an assertive personal style, have highly developed interpersonal skills, and is adept as an influencer and negotiator.

Responsibilities

- *Lead the surveying and evaluation of our existing technologies, and work with technical leadership throughout Blizzard to develop, implement, and refine our technology strategy, with a goal of increasing the speed and efficiency of development, reducing the complexity of developing and supporting multiple products globally, and improving the scalability and extendibility of our platforms and services.*

- *Develop and implement a progressive, long-term global technology strategy and roadmap that is capable of scale.*

- *Provide leadership on architectural decisions to ensure that the requirements of various teams and projects are considered and that the right technological decisions are being made.*

- *Ensure that technology decisions are being made throughout the organization that leverage existing technology where appropriate and are able to scale to meet future needs while placing value on the reduction of complexity,* **maintenance costs and downtime** *(maintenance costs and Maintenance downtime)*

- *Architect, design, and test new offerings, in collaboration with the rest of the technology organization.*

- *Evaluate* **innovative and emerging technologies** *(innovative technologies and emerging technologies) and make recommendations to senior development and executive leadership on the strategic use of these technologies.*

- *Industry thought leader who will articulate the vision in ways that will be highly valued by executive leader-*

ship and the broader gaming/ entertainment community.

- *Proactively participate in the acquisition, engagement, and retention of senior developers.*

- *Work with executive leadership to understand business drivers, market requirements, and competitive issues that may impact the Company's technology strategies.*

Requirements

- *Highly effective technology leader who excels in a quality-focused work environment*

- *Demonstrated experience leading a globally distributed, cross-functional technology organization*

- *Develop innovative solutions that meet the needs of the Company with a keen focus on functionality, performance, scalability, reliability,* deadlines, and adherence to development goals and principles

- Demonstrated success establishing streamlined software development processes

- Exposure to streaming technology, patching, testability, complex and scalable game engine, and graphics engines, databases, server architecture, and front-end/back-end web development

- Superb and persuasive coordinator, with both technical and business communities throughout the organization and externally with partners.

- Demonstrated experience developing effective strategies to build and sustain diverse, robust talent pools.

- Leadership and Management Behavioral Competencies

- The ideal candidate will be a team builder, team player, and a leader *with the personal drive, passion, and enthusiasm to both understand and successfully navigate a fast-growing company striving toward market leadership in an evolving marketplace*

- ***Highly analytical and structured thinker*** *(highly analytical thinker and highly structured thinker) with an excellent ability to put complex ideas into clear frameworks and to use data to drive strategic objectives and priorities*

- *A leader who creates loyalty, trust, and following. One who can energize people and teams and make cross-functional cooperation happen. This individual must be highly respected across all levels of the organization*

- *A combination of personality traits—collaborative, honesty, integrity, intensity, and passion—necessary to blend with the rest of the executive leadership team*

- *Able to challenge the team/organiza-tion while holding them accountable for their commitments*

- *A passion for video games and game development is required*

- *A compelling leadership style that includes exceptional people manage-ment skills, program manage-ment,* **business, and technology ex-pertise** *(business expertise and technology expertise) with a style that inspires confidence in some companies and their products*

- *Will solicit the involvement of others to build a sense of ownership. Must have the confidence to act quickly and decisively when the Company requires such agility*

Second Example of Edited Job Descriptions:

Group Controller/Director, Financial Reporting
Some Company
Some Headquarters
Finance
United States

Full Time
Up to 30%
1st

Some Company is one of the world's leading medical technology companies, and together with our customers, we are driven to make healthcare better. The Company offers a diverse array of innovative medical technologies, including reconstructive, medical and surgical, and neurotechnology and spine products to help people lead more active and more satisfying lives. Some Company products and services are available in over 100 countries. All qualified applicants will receive consideration for employment without regard to race, ethnicity, color, religion, sex, gender identity, sexual orientation, national origin, disability, or protected veteran status. Some

Company is an EO employer – M/F/Veteran/ Disability.

*Responsible for managing the financial planning process and reporting (**financial planning and financial reporting**) for the Neurotechnology Group to ensure overall accuracy and integrity of financial reporting within the Group. Responsibilities include partnering with the Group and Divisional leaderships team on various projects to help accelerate growth and improve financial performance.*

Duties and Responsibilities:

Financial Reporting

- *Responsible for all Group Financial Reporting: Weekly Orders/Sales Reporting, Flash, Actuals, Projections, as well as ad-hoc reporting for Group President, Group CFO, and Corporate*

- *Manage the **monthly flash and projection process** (monthly flash process and projection process) for* *the Group. Facilitate discussions with the divisions, analyze and summarize results, and present Group updates to Corporate*

- *Align best practices across divisions and Europe for all financial reporting, including aligning templates to fit Corporate, Group, and divisional needs*

- *Manage and facilitate the Strategic Plan and Budget process for the MSNT Group*

- *Financial partner for HCS, Flex, IMT, and ProCare Business Units, responsibilities include managing the budget process and projection process, monthly financial reporting and monthly financial analysis for the respective leadership teams*

- *Provide financial support and financial analysis on ad-hoc projects*

- *Attend quarterly Business Reviews to gain exposure to MS&NT businesses and processes*

- *Acquires, develops and presents relevant financial metrics, analyses and reports for internal and external audiences*

- *Support all President bonus administration; bonus scale setting and detailed review calculations for attainment/pay-out*

- *Manage, coach, and develop direct report(s)*

- *Business Development support*

- *Price-Volume reporting*

- *Review and support capital expenditure requests (CER)*

- *Competitor benchmarking and Competitor reporting*

- *Consolidation of the MSNT Group financials*

General Accounting

- *Review all journal entries, reconciliations, and HQ financial statements*

- *Maintain financial controls within MedSurg HQ to ensure compliance with Sarbanes-Oxley and compliance with Corporate Policies*

- *Provide financial support to HCS, Flex Financial, and IMT for projects and monthly accounting*

- *Review Hyperion Financial Statement*

Minimum Qualifications

- *Bachelor's degree (B.A. or B.S.) and relevant work experience in related field required.*

- *MBA and/or CPA certification preferred.*

- *Strong working knowledge of Microsoft office tools, strong accounting knowledge, understanding of GAAP and SOX preferred.*

- *Minimum of 10 years of Finance/ Accounting experience.*

- *Experience with financial system (Hyperion) preferred.*

- *Must be highly analytical, organized and possess a high degree of attention to detail. Ability to manage multiple requirements simultaneously and meet tight deadlines with a high degree of accuracy.*

- *Must possess the ability to manage by influence with accounting teams to ensure timely submission of data to Group and/or Corporate.*

- *Commitment to excellence and high standards.*

- *Excellent written and verbal communication skills.*

- *Excellent organization skills.*

- *Previous people management experience required*

Wordle.net – landing page

Wordle is a toy for generating "word clouds" from text that you provide. The clouds give greater prominence to words that appear more frequently in the source text. You can tweak your clouds with different fonts, layouts, and color schemes. The images you create with Wordle are yours to use however you like. You can print them out, or save them to your own desktop to use as you wish.

Create **your own.**

View some examples created by others...

If you click on the "Create" button, you get the page below.

Paste in a bunch of text:

Go

Wordle.net input page.

Copy your edited job description document and paste it into the box.

Wordle™   **Home**   **Create**   **Credits**   **Forum**   **FAQ**

Paste in a bunch of text:

```
1. relationship management and communication skills (written, oral,
interpersonal, presentation, etc)
2. leading projects and managing workload for simultaneous projects.
3. A team player with a great attitude and friendly disposition
4. software development lifecycle (SDLC) or software development is a plus
5. Project Management Professional certification (PMP) or other PMI
6. Project Management
Collaborate with internal team to develop and maintain project timelines and
budgets according to client contracts.
•       Understand project scope and effectively manage client expectations and
requests
```

Go

Once you have inserted your edited job description document, press the "Go" button as shown above.

You can see the JAVA pop-up below. Make sure you wait for it to show up. It sometimes takes a minute or two. Then hit the "run" button.

Above is the raw result of the word cloud. Unfortunately, it is relatively unusable in its current form.

The next step is to reduce the words to five, which should yield three sound words. Typically, you can get 20 good keywords out of 30 when using this process. I suggest that you use

20 good keywords in this process. You will see I only will cover one. This is just a repetitive process to get the 20 good keywords.

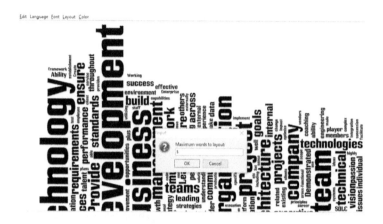

The next step is to make this more usable. Click the "Layout" tab and click on "Horizontal."

Click on the "Layout" tab, then click "Maximum words," enter the number "5" as seen above, and click "OK."

technology
team **business**
project
development

Above, you can see the top five keywords from the word cloud. There are two non-keywords: "company" and "business." There is one keyword that may be iffy, which is "team."

team **business**
development **leadership**
project **organization**
technology
management **company**
architecture

Above, you can see the top ten keywords from the word cloud. There are three non-keywords: "company," "experience," and "business." There are three keywords that may be iffy, which are: "team," "leadership," and "project."

Above, you can see the top 25 keywords from the word cloud. There are nine non-keywords: "company," "ensure," "provide," "organization," "people," "work," "success," "experience," and "business." Finally, there are five keywords that may be iffy, which are: "team," "teams," "leadership," "projects," and "project."

Navigation ▾ ✕

technology   ✕ ▾

22 results   ▲ ▾

Headings   Pages   Results

Has a passion for
technology

Support, Software
Development and
Technology groups.
Qualified candidates will
possess

Provide vision for
NanoSatisfi's technology
direction and
implementation given the
business

Build technology
infrastructure, architecture,
and requirements across our
satellite platform,

Rooted in technology know-

• → Provide vision for NanoSatisfi's technology direction and implementation given the business requirements set by the CEO and business development team¶

• → Build technology infrastructure, architecture, and requirements across our satellite platform, ground station network, and databases¶

• → Manage and grow our team of software development engineers, operations managers, and data scientists¶

• → Lead large-scale project management and project planning activities among the engineering teams¶

Solid execution experience — demonstrated ability to get things done, including multiple projects across multiple groups. Ideally this experience is related to building a data platform¶

• → Great team player¶

• → Rooted in technology know-how with a strong sense of business — able to fully grasp business relevant topics and optimize resource allocation to maximize business success, but have a deep understanding of technology and hands-on capabilities to be respected by the best technologists¶

• → Ideally someone who is passionate about next-gen technology, hardware, and space exploration¶

• → Specific technology expertise on the data-base side and ideally with an understanding of data from sensors or other Geo-Information Systems (GIS) to facilitate communication with the developers that work on hardware related technology¶

Above is an example of taking one of the keywords we identified in our word cloud: "technology." Suppose we put "technology" in the search box of our word processing program, in this instance Microsoft Word. In that case, you will see the occurrences of "technology" in your edited job description document.

As you walk through the document, you can see the modifiers of "technology." These can be used as part of the keyword pairs or keyword strings you can use in your LinkedIn profile.

Passion for *Technology*

Technology **Execution**

Technology **Direction**

Infrastructure *Technology*

Technology **Arena**

Technology **Requirements**

Technology **Architecture**

Technology **Leade**r

Technology **Organization**

Technology **Strategy**

Deep Understanding of *Technology*

Technology **Know-How**

Technology **Experience**

Technology **Community**

Technology **Groups**

Technology **Decisions**

The next step is to utilize these keyword pairs and keyword strings and put them into a spreadsheet. Evaluate "The Keyword Pairs Groupings" (rank 0–5).

Now put all your keyword pairs and keyword strings in the spreadsheet. You then evaluate the value of the keywords. You are allowed ten five-ranking keywords pairs or keywords strings that are the most important to you.

You then get rid of the looser keywords by ranking them zero. Most people do not use the one-rankings because the odds are you are not going to use them. So now you have the fun of choosing the two-to four-rankings. The fours should be relatively easy. The twos and threes seem to be the most painful to rank and generally take the most time.

Make Sure You Are Using Nouns And Verbs

You want to use nouns and verbs for keywords. If you are a marketing person, the keyword strings tend to be longer. The example spreadsheet is for marketing and general manager positions. Using more than five or six keywords in a keyword string is getting long and may need to be adjusted.

Track Where You Put The Keywords In Your Profile

When you place your keywords into your LinkedIn profile, you should track where you put them and your frequency of use. In the spreadsheet example, I never used the keywords more than twice. I do not recommend using a keyword string more than four times.

Test Keyword Placement With LinkedIn Search

After you place keywords in your LinkedIn profile, you should test keyword pairs by using LinkedIn search. Warning, a few keywords will search badly as stand-alone keywords. Do not discard them (such as Company & organization). There is a process for doing this testing covered in the *More Powerful Search Ranking book*.

The Most Important Keywords:

The most important keywords are your titles.

- Your Short Title: CEO, COO, CIO, CMO, CDO

- Your Long Title: Chief Executive Officer, Chief Operating Officer, Chief Information Officer, Chief Marketing Officer, Chief Digital Officer

---

This spreadsheet example is one that I utilized for a client. Please forgive me for obscuring the profile locations, but this is a working example where the LinkedIn profile made page one search for his position.

	A	B	C	D	E	F
1	Key words	Priority	Loc 1	Loc 2	Loc 3	Loc 4
2						
42	Direct experience in Board relations	2	ford			
43	Experience as a spokesperson to strategic partner organizations	2	dec			
44	extensive experience with P&L management	5	ford			
45	Experience in participating at the senior level in mergers & acquisitions	0				
46	private equity experience	3	heart	ford		
47	Experience leading a geographically dispersed team	3	dec			
48	Champions and creates the optimal client experience strategy	3	dec			
49	Client Experience Management	4	ford			
50	Product innovation experience	5	letna			
51	Demonstrated experience in execution excellence	5	heart			
52	Experience leading cross functional teams	4	ford			
53	Solid knowledge of standard research techniques and tools exp	0				
54	Product strategy	2	MY			
55	Familiarity with client experience concepts and optimization	3	Dec			

Example Keywords PDF

www.igniteyourLinkedInprofile.com/keyword
s

Chapter 9
Identify High-Value Areas of Your LinkedIn Profile

Donald J. Wittman, LI SEO, Search Visibility
Be More Visible on LinkedIn With a Search Optimized Profile
| LinkedIn Consultant | LinkedIn Training | LinkedIn Author

There are two areas of interest on the page view above that is the highest search value area on your profile.

First is your name line. There is quite a bit of valuable real estate after your last name in your profile's last name field. Do not put your last name in the LinkedIn first name field. This may cause problems for being found by name or translating your name fields. This is especially true when you submit your profile for a LinkedIn job opportunity. A name field is defined as all letters, not letters and numbers. You may blow up your job submission if you put something like your phone number in your last name field. LinkedIn does not permit you to put anything but your name in the name fields. However, it has become an acceptable practice to add degrees, certifications, and keywords after your Last Name, and LinkedIn has stopped enforcing it for now.

Second is your main headline field. This field is a 120-character field. The default entry in this field by LinkedIn is your title and Company from your current position. I suggest this be a keyword statement covered earlier. Your keywords in your main headline field may not rank unless they are in other headline fields.

As a reminder, be very careful about using punctuation in these two fields as well as the other headline fields we cover.

Your Current Position Headline

The top line of your current position is the next highest value field in your LinkedIn profile, as seen below. This is also considered your current position field. So make sure you have it in this field. If a recruiter searches using the current position or title search filter, this field is where it searches. If you have multiple positions with the same Company, your LinkedIn profile looks a little different than if you did not. This is shown in the first graphic.

Experience

 Wittman Technology, LLC · LinkedIn Speaker · LinkedIn Coach · Training · Consulting · Social Media
8 yrs

Advanced LinkedIn Trainer | LinkedIn Consultant | CEO | LinkedIn Training | Social Media | Speaker
2010 – Present · 8 yrs
Greater New York City Area, LinkedIn Consulting, LinkedIn Search Expert, SEO

I work with time-challenged executives on how to build an energized staff, improve employee retention, and ultimately become more productive and profitable by using the power of LinkedIn.

As CTO, I'm in a unique position to help organizations to effectively use LinkedIn to increase their market advantage. In 2012, I figured out a LinkedIn training methodology that can help just about any executive hiring manager find and hire the right talent, streamline the hiring process, and give back the time that they need to grow their companies. As a result, my clients have built energized teams, exceeded productivity, met revenue goals, and have increased their knowledge a... See more

CEO, Corporate LinkedIn Consulting, Corporate LinkedIn Trainer, LinkedIn Speaker, LinkedIn SEO
Dec 2010 – Present · 7 yrs 9 mos
Greater New York City Area | LinkedIn Training, LinkedIn Consultant, Coach, SEO

LINKEDIN CONSULTING

LinkedIn profile Consulting for Job Seekers:
1. Key Word Strategy & Identification... See more

 Wittman Technology, LLC · LinkedIn Speaker · LinkedIn Training · LinkedIn Consulting · Social Media
7 yrs 10 mos

Advanced LinkedIn Trainer | LinkedIn Consultant | CEO | LinkedIn Training | Social Media | Speaker

Wittman Technology, LLC - LinkedIn Speaker - LinkedIn Coach - Training - Consulting - Social Media

8 yrs

Advanced LinkedIn Trainer | LinkedIn Consultant | CEO | LinkedIn Training | Social Media | Speaker

2010 – Present · 8 yrs

Greater New York City Area, LinkedIn Consulting, LinkedIn Search Expert, SEO

I work with time-challenged executives on how to build an energized staff, improve employee retention, and ultimately become more productive and p̶r̶o̶f̶i̶t̶a̶b̶l̶e̶

Messaging

Advaced LinkedIn Trainer | LinkedIn Consultant | LinkedIn Training | Social Media | LinkedIn Speaker

Nov 2010 – Present · 7 yrs 10 mos

Greater New York City Area, LinkedIn Consulting, LinkedIn Search Expert, SEO

Wittman Technology, LLC - LinkedIn Speaker - LinkedIn Training - LinkedIn Consulting - Social Media

7 yrs 10 mos

Advanced LinkedIn Trainer | LinkedIn Consultant | CEO | LinkedIn Training | Social Media | Speaker

Nov 2010 – Present · 7 yrs 10 mos

Greater New York City Area, LinkedIn Consulting, LinkedIn Search Expert, SEO

Next LinkedIn Positions

One, two, three positions back are the next highest value fields. They should contain the name of the position you held and potentially equivalent position names. If you have room, you may want to put in the position you are striving to land.

If your LINKEDIN PROFILE was on PAGE 1 for your JOB SEARCH or BUSINESS, what kind of success would that bring to the table? LinkedIn is the best place for business people to find other business people.

As a previous CTO, I combine in-depth technology expertise toward the use of LinkedIn. I have a set of processes to get my clients found. For those DIY'ers, I offer a variety of Training Classes and Webinars to help you understand my proven process.

HIGH CHALLENGE JOB SEARCH

The most common complaint, after professionals complete their LinkedIn Profiles, is Head Hunters are not finding them on LinkedIn.

I help Professionals find the right "KEYWORDS" for the position they aspire to and place these words in my client's profile for the best search results.

This is only one of five metrics that are important to LinkedIn Search. This process results in significantly higher profile views and inbound contact rate.

JOB SEARCH PRODUCTIVITY

Another common complaint is they have a Highly Key Worded LinkedIn Profile and my profile views are still low, what do I do now?

Only about 1/3rd of the Head Hunters on LinkedIn have a HR Subscription which allows them to see all LinkedIn members. If LinkedIn Members can't see the other 2/3rd Head Hunters, they can't see you! Optimizing your LinkedIn Profile includes LinkedIn visibility, which drives Head Hunters or Business People to you!

CONTACT ME

I'd welcome the opportunity to schedule a time to talk about your LinkedIn challenges and explore how we may be able to work together. I teach seminars, workshops and provide one-on-one tutoring and coaching to clients looking to strengthen their presence on LinkedIn.

I can be reached at:
email - don@donaldjwittman.com
Telephone - 203-917-4258

About Field

The About field is the second from the bottom of LinkedIn value areas of your profile. It is just above the plain text. The fundamental importance of your About field is that it is the first field most recruiters or customers will see. So please make the most of it.

Skills & Endorsements

The top three to five skills help LinkedIn build the theme of your profile. It means that if you have CFO skills in the first five skills, it will help you in searching for a CFO position.

Having less than 25 endorsements for any skill will make those particular skills valueless.

LinkedIn has been playing with the search value of skills. At this time, they range from nothing when you have less than 25 endorsements to up to three points, but this ranking value is inconsistent.

Skills & Endorsements

+ **LinkedIn Training** · 99+

    Endorsed by Gary Arnold PhD (LION) and 6 other mutual connections

+ **LinkedIn** · 99+

    Endorsed by Sandra Long and 4 others who are highly skilled at this

    Endorsed by Eric J Christeson, PhD, DBA, PMP, SSCC, Author and 11 other mutual connections

+ **Linkedin Marketing** · 99+

    Endorsed by Gary Arnold PhD (LION) and 8 other mutual connections

Show more ∨

Chapter 10
Conclusion

You now have a lot of work to do to get your LinkedIn profile in good shape. It generally takes a good week of effort to get these tips implemented. In addition, the keywording of your profile can be a bit of a problem if you are in a challenging area, such a New York City, Boston, Chicago, Los Angeles, and San Francisco. In these areas, it may take several rounds of changes to rank for the position you want.

There are two situations where optimizing your profile may not be helpful.

First, some positions are highly sought after. Suppose the position you are looking for is highly sought after, and there are many more people looking for that position. In that case, there are positions available no level of optimization may help because of its competition. In cases like this, these positions generally get filled by people who are already known to the recruiters.

Second, there are just none of these positions available in your area. Not having a job position you are looking for in your area is becoming more common than not. Do not make your search too narrow initially, or you may be throwing away opportunities.

I wish you all the best in your job search endeavors.

About the Author

Donald J. Wittman is a LinkedIn coach, trainer, writer, and consultant.

For more than ten years, Don has trained over 100,000 job seekers, college graduates, professionals, and small companies on finding their dream job, next client, and prospective hires, using LinkedIn, the #1 social media platform for sourcing professionals.

Don specializes in helping out-of-work job seekers, especially high-level executives, find their next job and earn their desired salary. Instead of *chasing* employment, Don uses his very own *Pull Methodology* that captivates employers and recruiters to reach out to job seekers instead of the other way around.

Don also helps B2B professionals, coaches, consultants, salespeople, and lawyers, get more leads by optimizing their LinkedIn profiles using the same Pull Methodology.

To learn more about how to improve your LinkedIn results vastly, land your next job faster, or have more clients find you before the competition, visit wittmantechnology.com.

Thank You For reading My Book

I Wish You All The Success In The World

URGENT PLEA !

I really appreciate all of your feedback and I love hearing what you have to say.

I need your input to make the next version of this book in my future books better.

Please take two minutes now and leave a helpful review on Amazon letting me know what you thought of the book.

Thanks so much!!
Donald Wittman

https://amzn.to/3cuDVsN

https://www.amazon.com/review/create-review?&asin=1733805915

Printed in Great Britain
by Amazon

42179329R00098